Crocus debuts / Suitcase

The Seamstress And The Global Garment

Published 2009 by Crocus debuts / Suitcase

Crocus Books are published by
Commonword Enterprises Ltd
6 Mount Street
Manchester M2 5NS

Suitcase books are published by Shorelines
admin@suitcasebooks.info

Cover design and print by Tyme Design

British Library Cataloguing-in-Publication Data.
A catalogue record for this book is available from the British Library.

For my Mum

Acknowledgements:

kah kow was first published by Flax (2008) as a poetry poster: www.litfest.org/flax.html

Monsoon is an extract from: Monsoon: Six Plays By Black & Asian Women (Aurora Metro Press,1993)

Brides of Dust won the 1992 Cardiff International poetry competition and was first published in The Redbeck Anthology of British South Asian Poetry, (Redbeck Press, 2000)

Four Corners and City of Culture are extracts from:
Four Corners, BBC Radio 4 (1997)

Kali Mirchi, Barter, Genderality and Been-sprouts were first published in Fingerprints and Other Traces, Flax 005 (2007)

Indian Ocean was first published in
Putting in the Pickle Where the Jam Should be (1989)

Identity Song, Healing Strategies for Women at War, Red Wine,
The Seamstress and Stretches of For-get-me-knots were first published in Healing Strategies for Women at War, Crocus Books (1999)

Friends, Grafting and The Sky will be Closing in 30 Minutes were first published in Pendulum: The Poetry of Dreams, Avalanche Books (2008)

Avenue was first published in KISS: Modern Black Love Poetry,
Crocus Books (1994)

Thanks to Sarah Hymas for insightful editing and Seni Seneviratne for encouraging my awakening poetry spirit.

Contents

presence

i gift you evergreen stillness
mesmerising love that cradles you

i connect you to gathering insight
from the waxing moon

i bestow you to escape the restraint
of winter's incubation

i endue a Golden Eagle's feather
rebirthing the everlasting present

kah kow

mother-trees ghost for clouds
in the Rio Azul basin
a pod remembers its relics
lures itself into ripening

faded fingerprints scoop seeds
fermenting the bitter past
into the candied present   the future fictional
today oppressing tomorrow

a Blue Morpho flutters
appearing and disappearing
a revolution of ritual

on a copper skillet an allele slaves away
conching and blooming;
seeking to decode itself
unearthing antiquity

time simmers
is tempered like chocolate
devoted to the next moment

monsoon i

The birth of Maya
the beginning of time
I cannot see my growing
the new moon in my eyes.

Spring to summer
I shout and scream
can find no peace
everything is too big and small
at once.

The air is laden
with the heat of summer
and promises to the land
growth and change will come.

From the darkness of this cave
I wait noon to noon
for the moon-dew
under a lowering monsoon sky.

monsoon ii

The heavens have opened
first drops fall
plump and sated
absorbing the dry air.

From a trickle
to a torrent
the roads are awash
rivers swelling

and swamping
the dust of the earth
is reborn.

The heavens have opened
and my womb has shed her lining
flows endlessly.

The flesh of Durga
fighting for change
the hungry red earth heaving
and growing.

I cannot look at the sun,
or swim in the seas,
or speak,
or behold the altar fire
in my temple of Durga.

Drenched and laden
bloated and weak
I sense gravity
claiming my ocean of blood,
bringing me closer
to the earth
moon blood in my eyes.

monsoon iii

Winter comes
my womb begins again
to prepare me for birth
to create life
a fruit for each month.
I flow
with the seasons
create my own seasons
am surprised
when the rain stops.

The soul of Kali
flying free,
Himalaya, heaven and mountain.

Before death
Kali devouring time
and after.

Brides of Dust

There are rooms in Pakistan which avoid me, old stone houses
carved from exile. At night the stone transforms
and women's voices cry, their smooth skin blends
into sandstone tomb.

She wears red chillies in her hair,
walks thirty miles for water and returns
to find her children turned to dust.
The rain is an offering she has not received.
Death find places to talk to her. Her mother's songs
are her grandmother's dreams, her daughter's nightmares.

There are flames and silence in these houses.
The sandstone women are married
to death. An old woman painted my hands
like a virgin bride while I searched her eyes for a flicker of belonging.

Three nights and two cultures I wandered
in desert lands, dreaming of sandstone women in village
houses, digging for roots, tumeric and
religion. Her head is sprinkled with water,
cleansing she passes prasaed to her daughter,
two hands, blessing. In the mirrors
of her kameez she watches
the eyes of sandstone women narrow and close.

She remembers
her mother never cut her hair,
she remembers
it coarse and grey. She remembers the eyes
of sandstone women. She remembers three cultures,
two nights, that roots make a difference. In her first language
she learns to say mother, in her second home. She remembers
sandstone women. In her dreams she goes home with them.

The boundaries of land shatter memory,
there is no map to lead my family
home. They travel to voices
and words become death. The colour of my roots
makes me shout. I am located in earth.
my feet have no voice. I am located in sound. I walk into language.

There are marriage rooms
in this story. She has more language
than difference. She speaks root words,
looks for rivers in the desert,
knows places to die with sandstone women. Closes her eyes.

Four Corners

'Empire of the East' in bold letters on the torn rusty hold
of a once grand ship   now despatched
to a steel graveyard   its ruling days over

How can I have grown in the Second City of the Empire
amidst its decaying shell? Why does my heart split
with every panel that's torn from its structure?

Outside the Trades House on Glassford Street
I fancy mysel' a weaver o' the Weaver's Guild
I wind down the plaid streets connecting
Campbells to McDonalds   Stuarts to McLarens
a woman in a head scarf on Bothwell Street stares
at me   do I look lost?
do I look like I've na hame?

On Saracen Street I gaze up at the tenements
dripping with stories of Merchant Traders
an' immigrants wondering whether
I'm the product of a marriage of East and West
North and South   or something in between

An equinox
where day and night are equal
where the sun rises in Mumbai
and sets over Glasgow

City of Culture

along Saltmarket down Tobago Street
towards Lanark Road I stumble
across Shah's Groceries an' Bombay Bazaar   Eight 'til Late

In the dusty rows an' aisles lurk
Rajah Dhaniya, Haldi, Jeera, Mirch
Bolst Curry Powder and Tikka Paste
neighbouring Norfolk Sage and Stuffing Mix
Khyber Guaranteed Pure   Vegetable Ghee bordering
Ambrosia Creamed Rice   Mangal Tea Masala mingling
with Typhoo   Imperial Savoury Snacks and Karela in Brine flanking
Bachelors Mushy Peas

an' I'm at the checkout with a full basket of things I canny pronounce
don't even know how to use   an' the Indian woman on the till
says something in Punjabi I don't understand
so I give her ten pounds   take the bag an' run

down India Street with the west wind surging
through the empty barrels
the dockside blackened by unfulfilled promises
my tartan shawl wrapped tightly   shielding me from September

skinheads lined up on the wall of Jamaica Street
like unrinsed empty milk bottles
uncollected   sour an' gaping

a brick chases my heels   I don't look up   running
like the Westerly down the North Sound
my shawl flapping   an eagle taking flight

torn packages of   haldi, jeera, mirch
swirling behind me like the colours of Holi
Mangal Tea Masala an' Imperial Savoury Snacks
floating down the Clyde seawards   the eastery current beckoning

retching on the corner of Saltmarket
above me on the riverside 'Welcome
to Glasgow - European City of Culture'

kali mirchi

kali mirchi predicts the fall of nations

pursuing a palatable future
in the Malabar mangroves

her emerging flower spike
ripening red   climbing the coffee crop
blackened skin abraded to white
to pepper a jar of Pataks

hurry curry

rain heralds her arrival
she pours herself into the land
in the post office she discovers *Pataks Original Mild Curry Paste* and begins blending
the ready-made with the soon to be made
her grandmother's words sizzling you can't make a curry in a hurry

she lowers the heat and adds the paste in a hurry
imperialism gives rise to the recipe's arrival
resisting the way curry had to be made
dissension – the right to her roots on the mother-land
the Kala Pani and Sound of Skye blending
could she put haggis in a curry

could she resist her birthright of curry
would her grandmother's ghost know it was with haste and a hurry
of blending
that this soil felt her arrival
in the mountains and vales of this land
until in the earth's womb a pact was made

and on her table acceptable ready-made?
lowering the tone with her curry
giving her tolerability in this land
if *Tescos* could do it in a hurry
globalised food had its arrival
aisles of ready-meals blending

chicken and tikka masala blending
allegiances made
departure and arrival
of the colonial curry
judgments made in a hurry
about who can migrate to the land

harvest the land
through blending
and mixing in a hurry
until the recipe is made
a bastardised curry
makes its arrival

blending promises made
we land a new kind of curry
hurry to await its arrival

indian ocean

the sea travels from
Mandvi to Ganga Sagar knows
no cease-fire line or difference
between a European and an Indian
body, except the sea
knows me, my brown skin
travels from Mandvi
to Gangar Sagar unraveling
around the coasts of India
travelling from
the Arabian Sea to the Bay of Bengal
the sea travels across
oceans and does not know that one
country has ended and another begun
that the spices in Sainsburys
travel
that the silk in Liberty travels
that people travel
except the sea
finds their bodies
on her ocean bed
and unpicks their flesh until
they are bones
and only she knows where
she has hidden them

cottonopolis

glazed shipping holes blink reflections
glimpsing the undertow
an Indian woman in a floral cotton skirt
makes ones and zeros rumba

the Warehouse of the Western World
tramples meadows as a rural backwater
is straddled by the Merchants Bridge
and 40 shillings a ton becomes six

oak king posts and hoisting gear
preserved English heritage
mock her new found freedom
iPod Blackberry Wii   ingrained

canal arms grab barges
steer pilfered cotton
from Spanish West India Traders
into the Royal Exchange

standing on the canalside
her face ripples sunlight   becomes
threads of Guinea cloth unravelling
the binary of who she's become

Into the Intersection

We reject the urban crossroads
Circle the corners round until it's a no-go
Green the concrete with painted spirals
Let our children navigate the neighbourhood

Redundant storm-drains become bioswales snaking
The sidewalk rocks with lotus crowns
Our roofs harvest rainwater until the downspouts
Disconnect and there's no drought

Bulldozers become feet   pounding clay and sand into cob
Hands build and mould niches into a community kiosk
A place we can sit and read poetry and notice each other
Knit   weave and wear our lives kindly

We plant witch hazel in our food forest   become well
Garden ourselves into barrios
Meet on share-it-square
And exchange our inter into existence

identity song

there are city signs
around and the
motorway arrows don't
give me no home-coming welcome:
here on holiday?
no just living

a woman on the bus
with a mixed race kid
swears she's white her thick black hair
and masala skin defy her mother
pretends she hasn't
noticed
that the other kids at school
call her curry face
and throw
chillies in her eyes

you buy your jeans from
Southall market and
say you won't ever go out with
no paki boys don't want them
touching your charcoal hair
say you won't marry no
crimson powder parting on your head
and your black bindi means anarchy

my grandmother has an X
in her passport means
she won't tell me
no hand-me-down tales
for me and my grandchildren
if the phone line

ever connected she'd say:
stolen land
and now they've stolen
you from me

self portrait as a global garment

I am hung in the earth's wardrobe
woven with the sinews of a million dying brown-skinned babies
their eyes sequins glistening in every twist of sunlight
as I flick my white Indian silk lengths

on my belt mosaic mirrors become rivers pouring
opulent jewels from the land into the palm of your hand
every last drop of earth's moisture drained for your appearance

try me on for size   it's not one size fits all
I am too small for Western bodies bloated
by supersized dreams too large
for the skeletal frames of malnourished children in Lucknow

I am a tight fit stolen from the needle-scratched fingers
of Brazilian sweatshop workers

I drape from the hips in a melting pot of style
I am Armani haute couture

I am ready-made for Wal Mart
a tropical treasure
your passport to exotic shores

Friends

Sindy and Barbie
argued neither's plastic
legs could
sit astride.

Their pinched waists
were made
for standing
in kitchens
modelling
evening gowns.

Sindy could
abseil
Barbie's golden
mane got hooked
on guttering.

To the rescue
Action Man descends
on yellow wool
frayed
against
pebble-dashed
dreams :
Barbie amongst
the pansies.

Sindy galloping
to the rescue
lilac tutu
ripped on

scarlet rose bush
spying Barbie's
mud splashed
floral pinafore.

Sindy and Barbie
riffling through
Action Man's barracks
get away
undiscovered.

Barbie in khakis
beautiful locks shorn
Sindy in
bikini and boots
messengers dispatched.

don't

don't join the Rebel Clown Army, even though you were Coco the
Clown in a past life
do the washing up, don't, and make art from the mould on your plates

don't attract attention from the 'authorities', buy a TV licence and try not
to look suspicious at railway stations

do go on a diet,
don't, gorge on chocolate éclairs, spam fritters and full English

don't travel alone in India
do, but sleep with a rock under your pillow

do drink organic sparkling mineral water
don't, drink ten pints of larger and a bottle of vodka in a binge session

don't travel through rural Tamil Nadu at night for fear of bandits
do, the bus is hijacked, remember you lived to tell the tale

do use a beauty regime that involves anti-wrinkle cream made from
bats intestines
don't, and wash your dreadlocks in menstrual blood

don't cross the road!
do, be cross with roads carving up communities

don't catch their eyes,
do, look through their leer into the why

don't dress as if you're asking for it
do, and ask for what you need

do send healing light to the capitalist oppressors, thieves and rapists

do wish on rainbows, comfort eat, skive work and have sex in
aisle five of the supermarket

don't stay in bed all day
do, and change your life

healing strategies for women at war

one: leave knives on the chopping board.
two: fry your love in hot oil
until it reaches flash point.
three: stir yourself up
with therapy books on anger, pinch yourself
to see if you're still alive.
four: lay the table with friends,
placing them carefully. separate with
napkins, knives, forks and spoons.
five: cut yourself into thin slices.
six: bake your dreams until they carbonise in the oven.
seven: stew family photographs. remember,
comparisons and memories should be kept secret.
eight: feed your addictions with the guilt
of using broken biscuits as a base for your life.
nine: sprinkle (don't talk don't trust don't feel) into conversations
about happiness.
ten: devour emotional distress and wounds of others as your mirror.
eleven: boil yourself in the pain of leaving
every time someone falls in love with you.
twelve: ferment ginger wine kisses
until they burn your lips.
thirteen: use pancakes garnished with
Scotch Bonnets to stuff your feelings into.
fourteen: sift your desires through others' needs.
fifteen: ice sex with pink fondant
and lie about what you want.
sixteen: eat lotus root filled with Miso
and pretend you're healthy.
seventeen: make yourself
a packed lunch and leave home.

red wine

she eats holly berries and watches
the midnight TV flicker reaching for
crushed velvet to bring her
tongue alive keep the tears inside.

she sings Christmas carols in June
thinks of grapes fizzing in the sun
her bare feet on sour red lino stinging
falling into brown paper and dust.

she swims for hours
grape-skins in her ears
takes a ruby aperitif and lies
to you about promises.

she drowns in crimson dye choking
on pain and wanting irony
tastes like cheap vinegar
cochineal laughter burning her mouth.

she washes her hair in rosemary plaits it
winding the strands tight
grows roses and years becomes
fat and empty and forgotten.

spurn

he monitored her via her handbag
unearthing forbidden tampons
she crept with blood congealed thighs
stalking the cornershop for *Always Ultra*

he threw the unclean khana heart-ward;
boiling masala sticking her kameez to her
she held her scream even as pani cascaded
soaking her shedding skin

he improvised his strikes on her
and afterwards he made sure
she played snakes and ladders
afraid to throw the dice

for fear of winning and being
plunged back in the snake-pit

Aground

Her white hands burrow through atta,
she calls brown flour,
and he adds pani smiling
she says water, he namak
and adds the salt.

Her gold thread sari border shines
like her newly wedded laughter.
He taught her recipes and words and cast
Indian customs across oceans and floors,
she learnt to bow her head and hoist it only
for English parties.

Some of her children slithered from her,
clotted blood glazing her thighs.
Girl children showered down from her until
a boychild she thought she'd
delivered happiness, but nothing changed.

Her kheema learns to fly,
she scrubs the stubborn haldi from the walls,
it smiles yellow
like the May sun on her wedding day.

barter

I swapped a purple sports-bra for the first dress ready-made
didn't recognise myself as the skirt skirted the mirror-tiles
suburban Noida rattling in the mid-distance

In the second dress I was shrouded like a bluebell's bell
the seams were seamless fitted like a glove despite the lack
of measurements she said she'd dreamed of me naked

I imagine her in the sports-bra, its lycra pinning her breasts
to her rib cage, she told me she'd worn it in Defence Colony Bazaar
acquiring haberdashery in small newspaper packets tied with string

later I found a pink ribbon on an inside seam
an embroidered motif that grazed my navel
and I wondered what it spelled

genderality

1978
aged thirteen / i wear a denim waistcoat /
khaki small-collared shirt
knotted with a black silk tie /
my mum refuses to leave the house /
with me until i take the tie off /
i stuff it in my pocket and wear /
an imaginary knot; centre-stage

scene one:
throw me a life
buoy sailor, we living
in sink or swim times;
all mouth and no trousers
getting thrown out the ladies
for looking so sexy butch
she's a girl!
she's a boi with a toy
denied admission to Vanilla
she's a girl
looking straight / through me

she's all fired up on T
did i say she?
i mean he, it,
shit, we're crossing over, under / cover
agents for the gender divide
becoming them and finding:
recipes for bombs
measurements for inside leg
how to grow the hair / elsewhere
he's a faery boi / should be a girl,

grew his hair and tucked his cock down
her inside leg
what a drag, not popular like the queens / not cultured
like the queers, something in-between the word-play
translator or impersonator
transgressor or impresser
test the line

scene two:
skirts don't suit me, something about the cut,
the print, the way it hangs like abandoned washing
grazing my knees, bellowing in the breeze
an embarrassment / like the time I walked down
market street with the back of it all tucked up in my knickers
and I never knew / that I could wear genes
charity-shop retro, inherited from the underground
worn lives / gender uniforms on rails /
try them on for size / unwanted garments / on special offer /
shop-soiled
y change what you wear / to fit in with your x's crowd
you still won't gain entry / they'll be wearing top man /
when you're all tammy girl

scene three:
on the street I wear one of my off-stage identities
and an old lady says:'can you help me cross the road young man'
i readjust my sock / take my hands outta my pockets,
grasp her arm, dodge the 6pm traffic

scene four:
i can rip-saw / use a lathe, make mortise, tenon and dovetail joints
'tie your hair back' the journey-man says / health and safety
i plane oak, wafer thin curls peeling back to smooth contours, trace the
years with my index finger /
28 and still no sign of an identity; carpenter, film-maker, web-designer
activist, mentor, chairperson
gendered jobs / apply within

scene five:
write an application / person specification:
silver wisdom in her hair
roses / spirals / celtic knots
big / bouncy / / bra-less / breasts /
stunt cunt flying open
four armed lesbian kali gender killer
this flavour is not available in other stores

the seamstress

she looks up
the needle swaying
under the weight of the words
red thread scratching the
outer seams of a silk kameez

she can't recognise your
almond eyes dripping onto the cloth
your body has changed
become distorted
your tawny skin seems
different because it has lain
under a woman's hand

she thinks luckily she's
already measured your
breasts, your hips, your
inside leg because now
she doesn't want to put
her tape measured hand there

it's no longer
a woman's inside thigh
the measurement has

expanded
become an unknown domain
a terrifying territory

and now your clothes
are one size larger
the cloth hanging wide around
your breasts
your inside thigh
and your salwaar is so
tight around your ankle
you can hardly get them on

is gay a country?

I'm wearing a red wedding sari trying to enter
vanilla and the Black bouncer says:
'you're in the wrong country love'
and I wonder is Gay a country?

queuing for the ladies a Black dyke says:
'can you make chicken curry?'
and I contemplate is Gay a recipe?

on the dance floor a khush sistah says:
'you're brave wearing that!'
and then is shocked that I'm *'not fully Asian'*
perhaps that's why I'm fully Gay I deliberate

I leave early and taxi it home
as we round the bend the Asian driver says:
'what you wearing Asian clothes for?'
and i say:'cos I'm Gay and drop me off on the corner
I wanna walk home'

been-sprouts

break-up from your girlfriend, discarding longing into compost
you need to have prepared yourself the day before
pick-over and remove any broken feelings:
fear, anger, hatred
rinse in several changes of lukewarm water to remove
dust and anything left from the milling process
cover all with warm water and soak for twelve hours
put in a plastic bag that has been punched all over with holes
(you can do this with a fork)
place the bag in a sieve leaving the mouth of the bag open
cover this opening with a tripled well-dampened tea towel.
balance over a large bowl in a dark, draught-free place,
some people use the unlit oven,
or the area under their sinks
drain
try balancing your needs with hers
drain
you will find other feelings have sprouted overnight
let warm water gush over again and again and eat up
any excess emotion
rub your emotions carefully, that which doesn't float away
should be picked off.
repeat this process every four hours, never disturb the feelings
continue to do this for three to four days or until
the feelings have elongated
this is the ideal process producing perfect emotions
anything else will produce stunted results

at this point do not cover up your feelings, place in the fridge
and all will stay healthy for three days.

use to stir yourself up.

grafting

our love was quiescent
her tongue cut my limbs until I
was too pruned to last the first frost
I waned through winter
my rootstock reaching earthwards
bark peeling to mulch

all winter through dormant dreams
I thought about grafting myself
onto the body of her new love
imagined my cut limbs on
her torso frozen through solstice

after Imbolc a tear growing in her skin
my arms sprouting out
to hold my ex-lover again

Avenue

Blue, I turn cold beneath
the sheets, turn to you and
burn like the August sun. Sweet
sweat runs and pours and I want to
pour April rain into you.

Beyond the blue,
the red and gold wedding of distance.
I want to hold you, beyond the blue. I
return to yellow sand. It burns
my feet red,
the golden grains gathering
my heat grows.

She is a pirate and I smuggle
gold for her.
She journeys oceans and returns
to me. I give her rubies and she
gives me honey and watermelon. I am
sweet in the heat
and do not feel the sand
burning my feet. Red
and the blue
disappears to black.

I dream of her in Barcelona,
Avenue Portal de l'Angel,
from the shimmer of the street she rises.
She is September, October, November, December
blue. And I am
blue. Mediterranean blue.

stretches of for-get-me-knots

behind your step
is a moment waiting
for fortune undulating
into hazy places
where you unzip small breaths
along a narrow path
with the jagged angle
of your elbow to the sky
and tongue to belly in dusk's light
the taste disappearing
into islands which wash upon
their own shore
the weathered passion
of expectation

below your knee I see a hand searching
a rhythm beginning
a wish saturated
after it begins I kiss the cliff edge
knowing there are no lies
in desire
no half measures in willing
no places to leave undone

I lay open tied by for-get-me-knots and
the green
my fingers tear at clumps
your fist breaks into a palm
as you swim into whispers
sharp as the cliff edge
hanging hard and hot into
fenced reminders of how sand
was once rock

the sky yawns into dusk
blows fragments of your rapture
into legs snaked in embrace
I lie spread
a picture of plenty
a box unwrapped
and look where there is a whole stretch
of the cliff path to be walked

The Sky Will Be Closing In 30 Minutes

Can all clouds please collect their small fluffy ones
from the Sky Lark crèche.

Clouds must keep their misty outlines with them at all times,
unattended wisps of milky air will be treated as suspect
and destroyed by Mr Blue, head of Sky High Security Services.

Lavish yourself in To The Skies:
The largest supplier of clouds to be seen
above the line of sight.

Will a member of Sky Security please report to Mr Blue immediately.
Will a member of Sky Security please report to Mr Blue immediately.

Bargain-Cloud-Day:
Three clouds for the price of two on rainy Mondays.

The Sky's The Limit:
The biggest mass of apparent canopy over our heads
in the Universe.
Open 24 hours, 7 days a week.
Sky: for all your weather needs.

Will a member of Sky Security please report to Mr Blue immediately.
Will a member of Sky Security please report to Mr Blue immediately.

The Sky will be closing in 5 minutes.
Please make your way to your nearest exit.

Glossary – Punjabi

Prasaed – a blessed food
Dhaniya - corriander
Haldi - tumeric
Jeera - cumin
Mirch - chilli
Masala – spice
Kali mirchi - black pepper
Kala pani – black water, crossing of Indians to the UK
Tikka masala - A marinade made from various aromatic spices
Bindi - a forehead decoration
Khana – food
Kameez – Indian blouse
Pani - water
Atta - flour
Noida - the New Okhla Industrial Development Area, India
Namak - salt
Kheema - minced lamb curry
Salwaar – loose trousers
Khush - gay